MAKE EVERYDAY LIFE

THE LIFE OF YOUR DREAMS!

FULFILLING LIFE

PLAN YOUR PASSION

OWN YOUR LIFE

DAVE YARNES

visit: www.3cplan.org

Successful entrepreneur and businessman, Dr. Dave Yarnes offers a roadmap to the good life. His personal stories, practical insights, and clear vision help you set your own course to sustained, holistic prosperity.

Based on solid moral values and strategies for intentional self-analysis, this book will help you to define true success and craft a realistic plan for achieving your goals.

Don't waste another minute! *The Three Circle Strategy for a Fulfilling Life* is your guide to living the good life—every day!

AN INTRODUCTION TO THE

THREE CIRCLE
STRATEGY

FOR A

FULFILLING LIFE

DAVE YARNES

DESTINY IMAGE® PUBLISHERS, INC.
P.O. Box 310, Shippensburg, PA 17257-0310
"Promoting Inspired Lives."

This book and all other Destiny Image and Destiny Image Fiction books are available at Christian bookstores and distributors worldwide.

For more information on foreign distributors, call 717-532-3040.
Or reach us on the Internet: www.destinyimage.com

Edited by Sarah C. Godwin
Cover design by Eileen Rockwell
Interior design by Terry Clifton

ISBN 13: TP 978-0-7684-1832-3
ISBN 13 EBook: 978-0-7684-1833-0

For Worldwide Distribution, Printed in the U.S.A.
2 3 4 5 6 7 8 9 10 11 / 22 21 20 19 18 17

CONTENTS

Introduction 7

Chapter 1   Plan Your Passion, Chart Your
             Course, Own Your Life 15

Chapter 2   The 3C Strategy 29

Chapter 3   Before We Begin,
             Emotional Alignment 49

Chapter 4   Circle of the Spirit 65

Chapter 5   Circle of Skills 95

Chapter 6   Circle of Self-Mastery 123

Chapter 7   Keys to Maintaining a Fulfilling
             and Prosperous Future 149

Chapter 8   Love Your Life and Learn from
             Your Setbacks 161

Chapter 9   Proactive Visualization 171

Chapter 10   Parting Thoughts—Getting Ready
             for the Rest of Your Life 187

INTRODUCTION

Almost 20 years ago, I started teaching a seminar series which became the source for much of the research and material for this book. The lessons I learned while developing and refining the content have been invaluable. Perhaps more importantly, I have been able to interview hundreds of those who have been impacted by these lessons and discover what elements have had the most sustained positive outcome. I and others have been able to improve this material and its presentation to make it more and more effective and easier to apply.

The core message has been refined into three overarching master topics to create *The Three Circle Strategy* (3C Strategy), which I believe holds all the keys to developing a fulfilling, prosperous life.

THREE CIRCLE STRATEGY

MASTER TOPICS

- Circle of Spirit (flame)
- Circle of Skill (scroll and quill)
- Circle of Self-Mastery (compass)

Within each of these circles are steps to a life-changing plan of increasing prosperity and fulfilment. It has taken considerable time and effort to keep the core message simple, easy to understand, and easy to apply.

THE SMALL BOOK FORMAT

Considerable attention went into analyzing size and content for this project. I have a few goals in creating this small intensive book format on *The Three Circle Strategy*:

1. I wanted to make this book concise and condensed and have less intimidating size so as to open my concepts to more casual readers.

2. I wanted to create a physical copy that is small enough to carry throughout the day in a purse, coat pocket, carry-on, or

backpack. I felt it was important that the book not just stay on a desk or in a home study but could be read whenever and wherever there was a quick break. This portable style allows the material to integrate with life's various perspectives.

3. I wanted to make this version compact and affordable so it could be purchased as a gift to others. Whether to family members, business colleagues, customers, employees, and other reading groups, I have tried my best to make the content and size a gift I personally would like to give or receive.

If you received this copy as a gift, I am thankful to your benefactor. If this material is beneficial and thought-provoking, please consider buying additional copies for distribution as gifts to others. Let's keep the movement growing.

Before You Begin, Download the Free 3C Companion Guide

The Three Circle Strategy for a Fulfilling Life has lessons, as you're about to discover, that have helped many and are easily applied to your life on a daily basis. The *3C Companion Guide* is a free essential companion resource that is easily downloaded in moments and is both printable (if you're like me and still like paper and pen) or usable in e-format. The *3C Companion Guide* has expanded material for each section and contains corresponding questions which will walk you through simple, practical application steps. Each section of this workbook is designed to give you space to reflect. All this is designed to help you integrate the material effectively into your personal plan. You can download your free copy of the *3C Companion Guide* at www.3cplan.org.

PRINCIPLES—NOT METHODS

Have you observed how many people have a desire to change but most don't have a plan? Developing and maintaining a plan for a fulfilling and prosperous future can be one of the most richly rewarding activities in life. I will show you how to create your own life plan based on the 3C Strategy for fulfilment and prosperity.

Principles are universal truths and they are transferable. Methods, specific tactics and procedures, are often difficult to transfer from person to person. Principles can be applied regardless of your age, background, or current level of success. Your plan must be customized to fit just you. You will find that this single difference of applying true principles will become an important key to unlocking your potential and sustaining a more abundant life.

When you create the right plan to fulfill your dream and then you work to take care of it, it can grow and produce fruit you may never have imagined. No one intentionally plants weeds in a garden, but if you plant a garden and do nothing to care for it on a regular basis, weeds will grow. The same is true about your life plan. Sustainability, fulfilment, and true prosperity take some effort, but yield results that last.

What I write about here, I honestly strive to intentionally practice and live. Most of the significant positive changes in my life have come from understanding and applying the principles that lie ahead in these chapters. I hope your experience is as life changing as mine.

CHAPTER 1

PLAN YOUR PASSION, CHART YOUR COURSE, OWN YOUR LIFE

"Let him who would move the
world first move himself."
—SOCRATES

I still remember his question as if it were yesterday. I was sitting in Washington Reagan Airport, completely engrossed in a conversation with a great spiritual leader, my friend James Cannon.

Commuters rushed by in all directions, but I remember being so focused that it seemed as if the noise and distractions around us were muted. His question was big, and I knew I had not considered it in the past. I also knew it would help set the course for the rest of my life.

WISDOM OF LEADERS

James was well known for his incredible business and his philanthropic exploits. I was young, my companies growing and philanthropic efforts just beginning. Ever learning, I always looked forward to whatever time I could spend with him. I asked him about his success. I thought of as many questions as I could to throw at him on a number of topics.

Over the years, I have found ways to grab moments with key leaders wherever and whenever I can. If I know someone is traveling and has a long layover or is stopping at a certain airport, I often arrange my schedule to coincide with theirs, to grab a few minutes in their busy schedules. I had to sacrifice and be intentional, but it was always worth it.

My topic for the day with James centered on some orphanages that he and I had financially underwritten in East Africa. The need was immense. The AIDS pandemic was ravaging villages and creating masses of orphans. We talked about lessons we had learned. We discussed watching the children grow up to lead fulfilling lives. We remarked, as we poured money into this devastating need, that our personal bank accounts grew somehow miraculously, supernaturally.

A question about personal focus had been forming in my mind. I said, "I feel so passionate about the work in Africa, but I am also seeing incredible opportunity in business here in the States. Plus, my family is young and the travel is often grueling. There are so many directions to consider. I just want to make sure I'm focusing my efforts wisely."

His look seemed to intensify and he stared at me for a moment. Then he looked at his watch and glanced at his ticket. He continued in a more serious tone, "I have to run, but there is something I have wanted to tell you that seems obvious to me but might not be to you."

THE QUESTION

"You are at a crossroads, and it seems as if you are trying to go in a lot of directions, but there is really one question to be asked, and you're the only one that can answer it. Once you do, you will be able to focus your energy on making it a reality. Then every other aspect will fall in place naturally. When all is said and done, what will you have considered a worthy life?"

With that, he picked up his bag, we said our goodbyes, and he walked off to his gate.

The question was so simple but haunting. Looking backward from the end of my days, what would I consider a worthy life? What would be my measure of fulfilment and prosperity?

I want to challenge you to examine this question and similar questions. From their answers, you will develop the components for a clear, personal plan for your own 3C Strategy. As you continue, don't be misled by the simplicity of the material ahead— often the most powerful truths are the most simple.

TAKING OWNERSHIP

Research shows that individuals approach the topic of change and movement toward fulfilment and prosperity in one of two ways. There are those who believe they have no control over exterior conditions and are not able to influence or affect change. On the other end of the spectrum, there are those who believe they can change and control most aspects of their own environment. This second group has a strong understanding that they can dramatically influence their personal world through their actions.

The first group will be driven by circumstances and not by choices. The second group will live a more dynamic and for-ward-driven life. The bottom line is, the more influence you believe you have, the more things in your life you will try to influence and the more success you will sus-tain. Just trying to exert influence creates a higher probability of actually being able to make change.

As we get started in this life changing material, take a moment to adjust your thoughts. Attitude makes the difference between those who live their dream, feel ful-filled, and create the type of life they believe they were destined for and those who live at the mercy of their current surroundings and circumstances. Before you move on, pause a moment to think deeply about your atti-tude, and make a commitment to yourself to approach this material with a fresh sense of empowerment.

> When you undertake the task of uncovering and defining what matters most to you personally, a true, lasting type of passion and clarity will be released.

CORE PASSION AND CHANGE

You may have tried to muster this passion from time to time as projects and platforms demand. But if you're like most, when the moment passes or the project ends, the passion fades. Why? This type of passion is what I call "situational passion." It exists only in relation to a cause. However, when you undertake the task of uncovering and defining what matters most to you personally, a true, lasting type of passion and clarity will be released. Let me say it simply, clarity and visualization of what matters most to you will create a lifestyle of passion. This is what I have come to label "core passion" and it is a powerful tool for continuous change.

Over the years, in numerous seminar environments, I have asked the question, "How many feel they are in a season of transition in life?" Amazingly, 75 percent respond in agreement. However, when I ask for clarity as to what the next season holds or what the plan looks like to get there, inexplicably almost none can describe what this transition looks like.

If you will use the following questions in a deeper, more thoughtful way, I assure you profound clarity will follow. You may find the answers are far more challenging than they may appear on the surface. Pursuing honest answers will help you envision what your life will look like in your idyllic future. As you seek the answers, you will be able to refine your understanding of what changes must occur in order to get from where you are now to where you want to go. I assure you that your core passion will build.

Even from a casual consideration of the questions below, most people realize their magnitude and significance; sadly, many never take conscientious time to reflect on and answer them. The 3C Strategy for a fulfilling life will give you a framework to answer and act upon these and other of life's most important questions using  3C Exercises at the end of each chapter in conjunction with the free *3C Companion Guide*.

The material and questions ahead make the process simple and rewarding. This combined plan supports you as you plan your passion, chart your course, and own your life.

 3C EXERCISE

The *3C Companion Guide* (available for free at www.3cplan.org) has expanded material and corresponding chapter exercise questions. It is designed to give you space to reflect and comment, with exercises for further thought and application. It has a printable format designed to carry alongside this book. Use the 3C Companion Guide to record your responses to these and other ⚫ 3C Exercises and to journal and track your development.

- What really is important to me?
- What kind of person am I called to become?
- Who am I to share my life with?
- What aspects of life are the most important to focus on now?
- Which area of my life is most drastically in need of improvement?
- What specific changes would I like to see?

- After these changes are made, can I picture myself living in a satisfying lifestyle of fulfilment and prosperity?

CHAPTER 2

THE 3C STRATEGY

Over the past 20 years of my life, a simple but profound theme has come into focus. I emphatically believe the difference between fulfilment, prosperity, and effectiveness as opposed to disappointment and scarcity is not a matter of chance but of change. My experience has led me to believe many have failed to apprehend the fulfilment and prosperity they were destined for because they lack a simple strategy.

Over many years and considerable thought, research, and refinement, the three circles, which represent the three core areas of life, emerged as the key components of making a strategy. In every individual, the areas of Spirit, Skill, and Self-Mastery embody the essential elements that need to be perfected in the journey of sustained fulfilment and prosperity. Each of these areas are like interlocking circles, and as you can see in the 3C Map, it is clear each circle is interconnected. Each area interacts and interconnects in a rewarding and fulfilling life.

INTRODUCING THE 3C MAP

Overlapping circle diagrams are often referred to as Venn Diagrams. The basic concept of the Venn diagram is to clearly convey where concepts overlap and how they interwork. In the 3C Map, the three circles of Spirit, Skill, and Self-Mastery have overlapping areas with one another, and they represent the interconnected and interdependent relationship of these three areas. At the center they converge like a bull's-eye on a target.

While each sphere of Spirit, Skill, and Self-Mastery has their own unique developmental designs and characteristics, which you'll read about in the pages ahead, they remain interdependent and connected to each other. How many times have you seen high-potential people have great skill, but lack the self-mastery necessary to advance their career. Or consider a highly spiritual person that has incredible character, but seems ethereal and lacks the needed skill set for useful expertise.

It's been my observation that many resources have been developed concerning the individual spheres of Spirit, Skill, and Self-Mastery, but there is little talked about or written about the holistic, harmonious nature of fulfilment and accomplishment that arises when these three circles are developed in concert with each other. In the following pages, each circle is defined in its own section along with practical steps for growth, but for now let's briefly discuss them on a wide-ranging level.

THE CIRCLE OF SPIRIT

This is not a call to religion, at least as most would define it. This is the understanding and engagement of the universal spiritual truths that influence and shape us and our world. This is a call to examine how congruent we are with collective spiritual truths. The goal is to understand and guide our personal transformation through awareness of spiritual principles that govern our world and interaction with others. This is the embodiment of the Spirit Circle. Your development of this area is transcendent, existing outside the material plane, and is not limited by it. This circle contains the seedbed of truth: hope, compassion, peace, joy, and inspiration. This circle can only be developed as you connect with the divine qualities in yourself, God, and others.

I challenge you not to be apprehensive when we discus an ongoing spiritual relationship with God. I trust you'll find universal, transcendent truths that deeply resonate within your core being naturally. It's as though they had been there all along, waiting to be awoken. Growth in the Spirit Circle is foundational to your development within the Circles of Skill and Self-Mastery. Without this key component, even some of life's biggest accomplishments can seem hollow and unfulfilling.

THE CIRCLE OF SKILLS

Learning and breathing should end at the same time. The lifelong pursuit of ever-deepening skill is something that requires identification, focus, training, and experience. These abilities come from focused education and from repetition and practice. Someone once said "an expert knows more and more about less and less." Determining which skills need to be developed and how to obtain them is a focus of the Skill Circle section. When you plan your passion and chart your course, the unique, indispensable skills needed come into focus.

When you are young, you learn skills because you are under the authority of a parent or teacher at school. As you grow and mature, you need to initiate your own self-study and self-management to learn skills. It is essential to consider the array of possibilities in the Skill Circle. The purposeful identification and development of key skills will help you to narrow down and focus only on those essential for your personal journey.

THE CIRCLE OF SELF-MASTERY

Self-Mastery is the discipline of understanding and managing your personal actions, impulses, and emotions consistently in all you do. It allows you to "feel comfortable in your own skin." It requires increasing self-awareness and self-management. In order to effectively impact and influence others as well as our environment, we must first have self-mastery.

Personal Self-Mastery is expressed in the areas of personality, inward character, and interactions with others. It includes the set of qualities that make a person distinctive, especially concerning the qualities of mind, feeling, and persona. As we grow in personal self-mastery, we can navigate interpersonal relationships with growing ease. Our ability to evaluate, influence, and persuade individuals and groups takes on new proportions.

Due to the nature of self-awareness and self-management, the important and practical skills found in the Circle of Self-Mastery section are foundational to leadership and interaction with others.

WHY ARE THE CIRCLES INTERDEPENDENT?

You may have already experienced a high degree of fulfilment and effectiveness in your life. There is great potential for more. You may find you have disproportionality developed a single circle. What new heights could await you? Have you ever wondered how much additional fulfilment is available? There is an exponential effect when you develop all three circles of the 3C Strategy.

When individuals focus mostly on the Spirit Circle, they see life as mainly mystical or ethereal. They often lack tangible personal prosperity, focused solely on spirituality without developing vital Skills and Self-Mastery.

Mastery in the development of important skills can open the door for rewarding and fulfilling accomplishments. Whether the skills are self-taught, acquired through academic pursuits, apprenticeships, or concentration and repeated application, they create a platform for some of life's most enriching accomplishments.

What about overdevelopment or disproportional development in one of the 3C Strategy circles? Skills are important accomplishments and often the time and commitment to their mastery can be consuming. We have all learned to beware of the skilled person who is self-absorbed or arrogant in his or her own development and performance. They are blind to other areas of self-awareness and spirituality while over-focused on developing skills. This can lead to self-aggrandizement, self-promotion, and the inability to recognize that skills are a gift to benefit society.

Longevity in fulfilment and prosperity is enabled through the Circle of Self-Mastery. Without this Circle, individuals remain at a low level of Self-Awareness and can fail to actualize socially or develop in the remaining two circles. However, as important and essential as self-mastery can be, we cannot live in a state of perpetual introspection without outward action.

As you begin to learn, understand, and apply the principles in this book, it is vital to honestly evaluate what your three circles look like right now, and which areas in each Circle are most drastically in need of improvement. You will be able to make substantial changes immediately just by learning and applying the material. However, I have found, like many aspects of life, there are improvements in progressive layers—you add new thought processes and remove harmful ones in stages. This careful progression allows each individual to not only incorporate new skills long term, but also to "heal" from the surgical removal of harmful thought processes that were uncovered in the process of discovery and change.

The principles ahead must be coupled with your passionate and resounding determination to find the fulfilment and prosperity that is available to you in new measure; it is there right now waiting for you.

START RIGHT WHERE YOU ARE NOW

There is something about the illusion of life that the right starting point for a journey of change is somewhere ahead but not in the present hour. The right projected starting point will be "When the kids are out of school" or "After I land this new position" or "When I retire I'll have more time" or "After I finish college." The list goes on. However, the discovery of a lifetime is not somewhere far away in some vague place. Opportunities you have overlooked for years are hidden right in front of you, waiting to be discovered. The allure of a better starting point in the future is an illusion. You only have today.

Most of the time, what you need is right in front of you, waiting to be discovered. Time and time again, men and women feel they must leave everything and seek their fortune somewhere other than where they live, work, and play. They think it is impossible that their success could be close and obtainable.

Are you like others, so convinced that success lies elsewhere that you may fail to see that the very thing you have been longing to uncover is within reach? I challenge you to reexamine your life and see the potential resources right at hand. Planning your passion necessitates a starting point that is always right where you're standing today.

Unimaginable discoveries are waiting for you, right under your feet. Your life, your character, your personality, your passion, and your skills are unique and fit perfectly, like a key in a lock. The experiences, richness, and quality of life that you have been seeking can all start to unfold right from where you are now.

"EUREKA MOMENTS"

The material in the following pages has been selected based on its repeated ability to produce instantaneous moments of personal revelation, which produce lasting fulfilling change. Many aspects need continuous course adjustment and depth of understanding that comes from consistent application of steps ahead.

I have chosen material that, in my experience, has historically produced more "Eureka Moments" than any others I have come across. A Eureka Moment is the moment when a specific topic, thought, or chapter will cause an instantaneous revelation and change. The Eureka Moment changes you positively for life. It can't be unlearned. It is the catalyst that brings you to a moment of understanding that releases true revelation. In turn, it creates a much-needed paradigm shift that alters the way you will view the world for the remainder of your existence. Enter into the next section with that expectation.

 **3C EXERCISE**

- In your life, is there one circle that is underdeveloped?

- What can you do right now to summon the courage and open-mindedness to start right now to develop this area?

- Is there one circle that you have over-prioritized?

- What could your life become if you had mastery in all three circles?

- Reflect on and answer these and other life-changing question in the *3C Companion Guide.*

CHAPTER 3

BEFORE WE BEGIN, EMOTIONAL ALIGNMENT

"I don't want to be at the mercy of my emotions. I want to use them, to enjoy them, and to dominate them."
—OSCAR WILDE

Emotions fuel our motivations and change. Positive emotions can give you clarity, drive you to persevere, and inspire others around you. Unfortunately, negative emotions are also a type of fuel. They can parallelize us from movement, cloud our judgement, and hurt us and others when they are not bridled. Before we look at each Circle in depth, I want to discuss the key component of emotions as part of your 3C Strategy, so that you are working toward your own prosperity and success with sustainability.

My view on the topic of emotions and their place in our lives has changed profoundly over the years. I have come to recognize the dynamic role of emotions in fueling us to find fulfilment, wealth, joy, and the things that matter most in our lives.

It takes emotion to sustain the passion to meet life's challenges. The key is *mastering* your emotions and making them work for you.

EMOTIONS ARE FUEL FOR YOUR UNIQUE 3C STRATEGY

In my early years, my examination of emotions, their roots, and their interaction in everyday life led me to a strong case for stoicism—emotionless life. I saw emotions as something that negated logic and caused irrational behavior. I saw the presence of emotions as the absence of calculated thought and clarity. To me, emotions hindered the thinking process. Then, during my collegiate years, my strongest concentration was in the field of workplace psychology— discovering what motivated people and how to acquire higher productivity out of an organization.

In fulfilling this concentration, I had to spend a lot of time studying and researching abnormal psychology. I dreaded it. I would have to prepare myself mentally before I could read abnormal psychological studies. Reading the stories of broken personal lives, the overwhelming feelings I had of sympathy and compassion were hard to manage. Often, my sense of empathy for the subjects of the study was on such a personalized level, I felt as if I had some obligation toward them—I wanted to find them and help them.

I was convinced that somehow an emotional imbalance was at the core of their problems, and I thought if we could just eradicate the power of emotion in their lives, how much better off they would be. I viewed emotions as a detriment to a logic-filled life.

My, how I was wrong! I could go on for chapters about why my view of emotions has changed so drastically. However, for the purposes of our journey I am going to cut to the chase. Emotions are fuel that allow you to plan your passion, chart your course, and own your life. Your individual 3C Strategy takes on new importance in order to harness emotions to fuel your unique 3C Plan.

EMOTION IN SOCIETY

I am aware that many would negate the vital role of emotion because of societal misconception of the appropriateness of emotion in different social, spiritual, or professional settings.

When an individual is spiritually inspired, there can be criticism like "they're just being overly emotional." Many can be emotionally moved by a true spiritual experience, attending a performance or a religious service, or even watching a movie that inspires them to spiritual thought. It is a natural expression to be moved to tears or overwhelming joy when you are impacted by a spiritual experience or thought.

A CEO giving an impassioned presentation of a new product launch can be labeled as insincere, using emotion as a means to boost sales. Some would not rightly understand the emotion is linked to the years of product development and the euphoria of the final release.

Emotions are a natural, God-given, beautiful part of uncovering the treasures of personality and spiritual development within each of us. Examining moments in our lives of heightened emotion often provide clarity concerning what areas of life are uniquely important to us as individuals and in turn which areas to pursue.

EMOTIONAL INTELLIGENCE

Emotional Intelligence (EQ) is a term used to describe a mature level of emotional balance. EQ is the measure of how much you understand and master your emotions and identify and adjust to the emotions of others. EQ is often a greater indicator for predicting who will be a high performer, more so even than IQ or technical skills. It's amazing how the study of emotional intelligence has risen from a few articles beginning around 1990 to a significant field of study complete with a wealth of books, articles, and university courses today.

Increasing levels of maturity in emotional intelligence are similar to increasing levels of Self-Mastery. The first step begins with Emotional Self-Awareness. The degree to which you become aware of how your emotions look to others is a step toward increasing your emotional intelligence. Think of the last time you witnessed someone behaving in an emotionally unacceptable manner. In most instances, the individual displaying the behavior is unaware of their emotional state. How about a boss, leader, or statesman who delivers directives with a passionless, disengaged emotional quality, do we follow them?

EMOTIONAL FEAR CAN KILL ADVANCEMENT

If you were to keep a detailed record of the various thoughts and emotions that go through your mind in a week's time and arrange them categorically, you may be astounded to see how many of your thoughts are wrapped around fears, especially fear of things that never come to pass! Certainly, there are instances where fear is a heathy, appropriate response. To actualize, we need to distinguish between legitimate fear and fear that causes dysfunction.

MASTERING THE EMOTION OF FEAR

In order for an object to be legitimately fearful, it has to possess two distinct characteristics. *It has to be present, and it has to be potent.*

If a woman, sitting in an office, is suddenly afraid of a spider, her fear may or may not be legitimate.

If her fear is based on the thought of a spider that is not present, then we could say she has a phobia or paranoia, and her fear is not legitimate.

If there is a spider present, but it is a toy spider that has surprised her, that fear is based on an object that is *present*, but because the spider is fake, it lacks *potency*. The fear is still not legitimate.

However, if the spider she encountered was both real and poisonous, having both *presence* and *potency*, then her fear would be legitimate.

Many people spend vast amounts of time in worry and anxiety over fears that are neither present nor potent.

- Fears can cause people to avoid social situations that could advance their career.

- Fears may prevent, entrepreneurs or investors from taking risks that could lead to enormous achievement.

- Fears can keep us from healthy change.

- Fear is the enemy of creativity.

- Fearful emotions can be transmitted to others, causing them to react to us in undesired ways.

Your fears can become ties that bind you and keep you doing things that are safe and familiar. They can hinder you from exploration and change. Fear will keep you from stepping out and taking risks that produce change and unleash the potential for fulfilment and prosperity in your life. Fears and anxieties can be so deeply rooted that even when you are enjoying great success, your state of mind doesn't allow you to take the needed time to recognize and celebrate the accomplishment. Decide now to reject illegitimate fear as you plan your passion and chart your course to a fulfilling and prosperous life.

FEAR AND ROOTED NEGATIVE EMOTIONS

Think of a young person who overheard their parents continually arguing about money throughout their childhood. Over time, that person could develop deep-rooted negative emotions associated with the topic of money. Their painful emotional links could cause them to avoid legitimate conversations about finances and keep them from being as successful as they could be. If left unchecked, these negative emotions can produce what some call self-sabotage. Behavior is deemed self-sabotaging when it thwarts us from a path of success, creates problems, or diverts us from our desired goals.

If we connect positive emotions to negative habits, they can also be used to reinforce unproductive habits. When I was young, my mother would often answer all of my life's disappointments by cooking or baking something for me. Over the years, eating when I was emotionally down became a habit loop. My emotional mind associated the comfort of food with the love, nurturing, and affirmation of my mother.

It's easy to see the importance of recognizing and changing these emotional connections. Learn to recognize and reject illegitimate fear, and self-sabotaging emotion.

 ## 3C EXERCISE

- What has been your view of emotions and their role in life?

- In the past, have your emotions helped or hindered your progress in obtaining life's most important goals?

- What are some of the lingering fears in your life? Are they legitimate? What personal measures can you take to overcome them?

- How can you begin to use your emotions as fuel for your dreams?

By now, your *3C Companion Guide* is starting to become an important resource for review of the answers to these and other important questions. If you haven't started using the *3C Companion Guide*, please consider it. It is available for free at www.3cplan.org.

CHAPTER 4

CIRCLE OF THE SPIRIT

"We don't have a soul. We are a soul. We happen to have a body."
—C.S. Lewis

Very few things are common across all audiences and all cultures. I believe there are three desires that are shared by everyone. We all have a need to be loved. We all want our lives to matter and count for something. We all possess an eternal component that longs to connect with God. Without this last spiritual connection, other pursuits become hollow and lack meaning.

Every person I have ever met wants their life to be significant and impactful. I have also observed, no matter how successful that person's life is or how vast their accomplishments, without a meaningful spiritual connection, their life is somehow empty.

Truly, this is not a call to religion as most would define it, this is the understanding and engagement of the eternal and universal spiritual truths that influence and shape ourselves and our world. This is a call to examine our response and congruency with these transcendent truths.

> Intuitively, each of us senses that we possess eternal attributes.

YOU DID NOT EVOLVE

You did not evolve from meaningless base elements of this earth— you were created. Your connection with your creator is foundational for a life of impact and meaning, a life of fulfilment and significance.

Intuitively, each of us senses that we possess eternal attributes. Whether this is defined as a soul or a spirit, universally there is a sense of an eternal component that connects us to God spiritually.

As a child, I remember in grade school being introduced to the reality that the universe is infinite. This was a big thought and a little overwhelming. Simultaneously, there was a deep internal realization that somehow I was connected to this infinite universe. I knew this intuitively. As one person put it, "there was eternity in my heart."

Since that time, I have learned the God of the universe is powerful, infinite, and vast beyond human comprehension. But somehow, further, God has great love. Even though God has incomprehensible authority, God is deeply interested in the smallest affairs of life. So how does spiritual life develop? Like all aspects of our life, we grow.

You don't have to be a devout religious person to grow and flourish spiritually. Neither do you have to be overly educated in spiritual matters. It begins by understanding universal spiritual truths that influence and shape ourselves and our world. Faith, gratitude, and reciprocity are just a few. Prayer, meditation, and contemplation are often our response to these spiritual truths.

Your development of this area is transcendent, existing outside the material plane and so not limited by it. This circle contains the seedbed of truth: hope, compassion, peace, joy, and inspiration. It helps us to differentiate between the temporal and things of eternal value. This circle is developed as you connect with the divine qualities in yourself, God, and others.

Without the Spirit Circle, this book is just about human psychology and skill development. As important as these two components are, they cannot take us to our highest destiny on their own. We could miss the experience of true fulfilment that comes from a true spiritual connection and inspiration. Through spiritual enlightenment, we gain ultimate perspective and new awareness of the purpose for life.

HOW AA FOSTERS CHANGE

Change is hard. Change without God is often impossible. Perhaps the most noted and most influential of institutions to understand the role of the Spirit Circle and its influence in creating powerful change is Alcoholics Anonymous (AA). I don't believe there is another single institution, cathedral, or temple that can lay claim to the amount and depth of changed lives to the degree AA can.

Advanced alcoholism is a debilitating and cancerous condition that drastically affects not only the life of the individual but also all of their personal interactions. For centuries, the unbearable effects of alcoholism were thought to be incurable. However, in 1935 in Akron, Ohio, Bill W. (a New York stockbroker) and Dr. Bob S. (an Akron surgeon) achieved lasting sobriety. They had both been long-time, hopeless alcoholics, but they were miraculously able to reach and maintain an alcohol-free lifestyle. Their highest goal became to help others along this path.

They established the steps and concepts that would eventually be developed into AA. As part of their process, there was no church to join or catechism to follow, not even the simplest definition of religious context. Instead, they emphasized the simplistic approach to acknowledging a personal connection to a higher power.[1]

Millions of lives have been transformed through AA, going from failure to fulfilment through their steps. The first three steps focus on spiritual truths and connections to universal spiritual principles:

1. I admit I am powerless over alcohol—that my life has become unmanageable.

2. I believe that a power greater than myself could restore me to sanity.

3. I make the decision to turn my will and my life over to the care of God as I understood Him.[2]

THE COMMON STORY

As I interact with thousands each year who often share their story of personal transformation, I am amazed at how many state an identical narrative concerning the discovery of spiritual truths. Although the stories may have different characters and various conditions, they closely follow a similar plot line. It goes something like this "I was helpless, at the end of my rope; I felt I had reached rock bottom. At that time, I felt an irresistible force telling me there was a God. I cried out to God, even though I didn't fully understand or believe, and my life radically changed forever."

The areas of desperation change. Sometimes there is an addiction, sometime there is a loss of family, other times it's financial collapse, but whatever drives the individual to this desperation, the heart of change becomes the deep acknowledgement of the need for God. When all human effort has failed, there is the ultimate surrender and appeal to God.

When we come to a point of deepest despair and desperation, this condition creates clarity that strips away any desire for trite or superficial answers. Maybe your life is not ravaged by alcohol, but are there other areas beyond your ability to change? Is it your marriage? Another addiction or habit to which you are powerless? For many, it might be a sense of emptiness and lack of true meaning, direction, and purpose in life.

Maybe deeper fulfilment, peace, and direction, have evaded you.

Innermost fulfilment, more than you have ever imagined, starts with the three simple steps, similar to AA. One, we admit that without spiritual help, we are powerless over certain aspects of our lives. Two, we believe that a power, a divine influence that is greater than ourselves can lead us to true, lasting, fulfilling lives. Three, we make a decision to align our lives with divinely inspired truths we discover through this humble acknowledgement. We begin to shape our lives cooperatively with a spiritual connection to God.

Let me say emphatically you do not have to reach rock bottom before this spiritual acknowledgement and transformation takes place. You can start today. Often, our pride and self-reliance keep us from this simple conclusion: you need God's help. It just seems, unfortunately, that it takes dramatic events before this becomes our conclusion.

DEFINITION OF SUCCESS IN THE CIRCLE OF SPIRIT

The definition of success in the Spirit Circle is different from the other circles. Success here opens the opportunity for success in every other arena of life. In the Spirit Circle, God interacts. This interaction creates the supernatural environment where your spirit can develop. In this transcendent realm, free from constraints of the material universe, you can remain unshaken by daily challenges as you build your skills and develop your character. Your prosperity and fulfilment take on new dimensions and definitions. When all around you is in turmoil and no one knows where to go, you are the one with the wisdom, peace, and stability to lead the way. This comes from your strong spiritual development.

Volumes have been written on this subject. It has been my experience that spirituality is deeply personal. I can't think of a more intimate personal topic than that of the spiritual connection to a God who knows and shares all our deepest thoughts and fears. For this very reason, this is the preeminent circle in the 3C Strategy and, for this reason, it is placed at the top of the 3C Map. The spirit is the eternal part of a person that has the ability to connect them to their creator.

> We all have a driving need to connect with God spiritually. Without this connection, the other pursuits can become meaningless.

SPIRITUAL STRENGTHS

From the time you became able to comprehend direction from others, your early years of life were centered on strengthening areas of personal weakness. You were assisted in your development from birth by caregivers who, for your own survival, begin to teach you how to grow out of your weaknesses.

As you grew, you moved from learning basic survival and locomotive skills to discovering a world of information and tasks you knew nothing about. From the encouragement to walk and develop as an infant, to lessons at grammar school, all of your early education was centered on strengthening your weaknesses.

Sometime during these years, you became aware that you no longer needed to focus on areas of weakness, but it was time to develop your strengths. The 3C Spirit Circle is where you identify and build on your unique spiritual giftings or strengths.

Most people do not have a plan for developing their spiritual strengths. Individuals have strong spiritual attributes in a similar way that they can have strong physical or mental attributes. You may have strengths in compassion, intuition, kindness, encouragement, or strength for sharing your faith. You may have spiritual strengths that allow you to sense the needs of others around you. Discovering these strengths and engaging in activities that develop these strengths is crucial.

Imagine a seven-foot high school student with a love for basketball who knows he has no skill in other sports. If he neglected developing his strong basketball skills because he spent time trying to do better in other sports, we would think he was wasting his potential. In most high schools, there are entire classes devoted to high-performance thinkers so they can invest more time in developing their already high-level intelligence. This is something that we should also be doing in the spiritual arena. We should discover our strengths at an early age and work on developing those strengths and finding the environment where we will thrive.

I believe a plan to find that place where your spiritual strengths flourish is vitally important. There are all kinds of plans for personal spiritual development. You need to create the one that fits best for you. I have made portions of my personal spiritual plan and the fundamental belief behind it available at my website, www.DaveYarnes.com in my Spiritual *Life Application Guide*. I am passionate about my beliefs, but I only share them as a source of reference. You must develop your own individualized plan.

MAKE A PLAN

Like other areas of life, I highly recommend developing a customized personal spiritual plan. Without some focus, priority, and intentionality, the 3C Spirit Circle can be the first area of life to be neglected. Life is busy and often filled with distraction. Don't get so caught up in the cares, worries, and business of life and fail to develop its most important components.

Your plan could include a daily time of quiet contemplation and reflection on God and his divine attributes, a time of truthful conversation or prayer, or a journal of your progress and understandings. Importantly, you might develop a list of activities you feel divinely inspired to participate in, like reading an uplifting spiritual book. You could set aside time for helping and showing compassion to others, such as visiting a homeless shelter or a nursing home for the sole purpose of showing compassion. A spiritual plan can help you become free from anxiety, and your life can take on a new purpose. You may have been a long-time practitioner of these or similar activities or this may be the first time you have decided to provide the needed time or attention to spiritual growth. Avoid comparison with others. You are spiritually unique and your 3C Spirit Plan is bound to be unique.

Through this process, continued spiritual enlightenment takes place. There comes a response in our pursuit; we call to God and he answers. Whether through divine intervention, a peaceful inner voice, miraculous circumstance, or a small ever-increasing sense of God's presence, he responds and guides.

YOUR SPIRIT AND YOUR MIND

Your internal thought life moves at an astounding rate of 600–700 words per minute. It takes proactive steps to focus this rigorous state of mind on working to your advantage. The mind is continuously being filled, either passively or actively, by influences that surround you at any given moment. Your mind and Spirit are interconnected and both are nourished by what we focus on.

I cannot overstate the importance of recognizing that every day you are being educated and your mind is being filled with something, whether you consciously choose it or not. You are either selecting the content and actively controlling your thoughts by a process I call "Active Meditation," or you're allowing your mind to be overrun by outside influences. It is important to take the time to consider your thoughts and to learn how to manage what you allow to fill your mind and affect your spirit.

MEDITATION PRACTICES THAT STRENGTHEN OUR MIND

There are several different views when it comes to managing the mind and thus affecting your spirit. Some of these practices are detrimental. One example is mind-emptying, which is a familiar concept at the root of many occult practices. I don't believe chasing out negatives and blanking out our minds is a helpful process.

I do believe the concept of mind renewal and "Active Meditation" significantly aids fulfilment and true prosperity.

You are responsible for all actions related to the control center of your thought life. This should be guarded as it touches your

3C Spirit Circle. You should never abdicate control of your mind, will, or emotions. If you do, it is a starting point for disorienting thoughts. An empty mind with no self-management can have negative side effects, such as confusion, burdens of fear, and disorientation.

Without strengthening the mind by actively filling it, the control and volition of the mind begins to weaken and atrophy. This can happen through neglect, or even simply indulging too much media or entertainment. I believe there is an actual loss of natural intelligence when the mind is not actively strengthened.

God gave each person sovereignty over their minds. Spiritual betterment of your mind is a process of actively filling it more and more with right thoughts as opposed to passive entertainment or blanking it out for the sake of a mystical spiritual experience. This is a critical differentiation.

ACTIVELY FILLING THE MIND

Your mind needs to be constantly renewed and fed. This in turn nourishes your Spirit. Your focus should be a lifetime journey, filled with true fulfilment and prosperity, characterized by healthy spiritual growth. You are the vigilant guard over your mind. Imagine guards at the gate of an ancient fortified city who momentarily hold captive, at the point of a spear, every traveler, tradesman, or foreigner who tries to enter the city. These guards carefully inspect all baggage and motivations before allowing entry through the gate.

If left unguarded, the mind will be filled with whatever is readily passing through your life at any given moment. Entertainment and social media can be great sources of information and inspiration, but they can also be a waste of precious time, or worse, they can give place to negative thoughts, fears, greed, and the like. Stray thoughts will, at best, just keep you from peace of mind and may even lead to losing focus on your passions for the future. The process of taking every thought captive is to actively choose what to focus on and also to actively decide what sources are not worth your time.

I have found it especially helpful not to overthink or wrongly interpret correspondence. Jack receives an email from Ray but it is short and the tone is direct. If Jack is not careful, his mind can quickly turn negative. "Ray didn't like what I had to say, and now he's angry, how can I fix this?" Nine times out of ten, you misinterpret and enable negative unproductive thought streams. Chances are Ray was just in a hurry and didn't reread his email.

ACTIVELY MANAGED MEDITATION

Your mind is a vacuum waiting to be filled with healthy thoughts. I am convinced that the way to fill a healthy mind, and in turn positively charge your spirit, is to undertake an active process of filling it with good things—satiating it purposefully and actively. This is an active mind process, not a passive one. It is a curriculum designed by you under the authority and inspiration of God. In this active process, negative aspects become diluted and you receive amazing, positive benefits.

Take active authority over the condition of your spirit. Make a plan for daily Active Meditation. Active Meditation seeks to fill your mind with good, pure, and honorable things such as thinking about the loving aspects of God, imagining your future accomplishments, or believing for a life that contributes and benefits others. When we rehearse these and imprint them, positive thoughts become second nature, even when you are met by negative challenges. This, in turn, produces an abundant soul or inner spiritual connection to God.

Mind-enhancement practices that come from popular sources, fads, or quick-fix schemes often lack essential spiritual principles for fulfilment. They can be harmful and fall heavily into two ditches.

1. They pervert the search for true fulfilling prosperity by stirring up greed-based motivations (money, power, things).

2. They lean heavily on dangerous mysticism and occult practices that call you to empty your mind and relinquish personal sovereignty and proactivity.

SPIRITUAL FORCES

I want to say a brief word about negative spiritual forces. I don't like to dwell on such things, but they are a reality. Without this view, we place the blame for effects in our own life and those around us wrongly. We all can be influenced by malevolent spiritual forces. Our beings have a spiritual component that is vital and capacious. Negative spiritual influences work together to distract and defeat individuals from true fulfilment and true spiritual reality. If you find interaction with certain individuals or visiting certain places or having exposure to certain media produces unwholesome, anxious, or fearful reactions, consider taking action to eliminate this exposure.

INTERNAL NEGATIVE VOICES

The internal voice of negative spiritual influence seldom speaks in the third person. Not often does it say, "Dave, you're no good, you're a failure, no one loves you, you should stop your pursuits now before things go wrong." No, in a much more subtle, malicious, and sadistic manner, the voice is disguised to sound like your voice. You will think, "*I* am no good, *I* am a failure, no one loves *me*, *I* should stop *my* pursuits now before things go wrong, *I* am a failure and should give up now."

I find there are two main misconceptions that come from negative spiritual influence. The first tries to get you to focus on every bad, negative aspect of your life continually, to produce constant thoughts of failure, guilt, and regret. The second asserts that God is angry with you and wants to punish you or God is too distant and can't be appeased. Because of this, it is imperative to develop the Spirit Circle of the 3C Strategy, using the information in the *3C*

Companion Guide. It will bring truth and clarity and begin to silence any negative spiritual voices.

 ## 3C EXERCISE

- What has been your pre-dominate view of personal spirituality?

- Have you identified your spiritual strengths? What are they?

- What does continual growth in the Spirit Circle look like to you?

Develop a spiritual action plan for your life:

- Active Meditation

- Reading spiritually nourishing and uplifting resources

- Talking with God/Prayer

- Listening for the voice and direction of God

ENDNOTES

1. All historical information concerning Alcoholics Anonymous is from http://www .aa .org/pages/en_US/historical-data-the -birth-of-aa-and-its-growth-in-the-uscanada.

2. AA Steps modeled from information on www.recovery.org/topics/alcoholics -anonymous-12-step/.

CHAPTER 5

CIRCLE OF SKILLS

"The Lord has filled Bezalel with the
Spirit of God, giving him great wisdom,
ability, and expertise in all kinds of
crafts. He is a master craftsman."
—EXODUS 35:31-32 NLT

This quote is from both the Christian Old Testament and The Hebrew Torah (as stated in the Pentateuch), and I find it extraordinary for many reasons. It is the first instance in both documents where the concept of being filled with "the spirit of God" is mentioned. More significantly, this unusual power was given to enable the head craftsman to have the proper skills for the construction of the Temple of God. For this incredible undertaking, Bezalel needed a culmination of all three circles for this major work of construction and design with precious metals and gems. This is an amazing example of how the three circles of Spirit, Skill, and Self-Mastery work together synergistically.

It would seem more appropriate that the first mention of this remarkable infilling of the God's Spirit should be in reference to performing miracles, or extreme missionary sacrifice, or remarkable preaching. Instead, in this ancient text, the Spirit of God fills a worker who has a great task before him, so that he can have the necessary mastery to do his work with excellence. This underscores the importance of interplay between the three circles in the 3C Strategy for a fulfilling life.

As stated earlier, a skill is something that requires training and experience that comes from focused education as well as repetition and practice. Our skills are developed through continual, intensive effort. These skills have both a physical and mental component.

Think of a master carpenter. The final pieces he creates are perfect examples of his workmanship. You could inspect and marvel at how flawlessly and skillfully his finished pieces have come together. If you were able to watch him as he labored, you would notice a quick and deliberate pace. A master carpenter completes tasks much quicker than an apprentice. His expertise grows and is shown through his finished work.

This is the nature of skill development. Through the development of skill in accounting, masonry, or public speaking, etc., our finished projects reflect our expertise.

To gain this expertise in a certain skill, it is often necessary to narrow your scope of concentration. You see this often in the medical community where the complexity of our anatomy requires doctors to narrow their focus and become a specialist in a certain component of medicine.

The powerful combination of training, repetition, and practice, along with an ever-narrowing scope, is what truly develops expertise.

> Be intentional about identifying
> and focusing on personal skills
> that have the greatest potential.

YOUR UNIQUE SKILL SET

There is no rite of passage or ceremony where someone says, "It is now time for you to primarily focus on your individual strengths and skills." I wish there were such a moment.

Initially, your understanding of your unique skills and personal abilities might not be highly defined or even noticeable. However, I guarantee that you will achieve more success in your field and enjoy more of the life that you are destined to live if you can be strongly intentional about identifying and focusing on personal skills with the greatest potential. This focused approach is fundamental as we plan our passion, chart our course, and own our life.

Identifying your individual strengths and skills and the areas where you have the ability to achieve exceptional mastery can be a significant journey. In fact, it will take purposeful, focused effort on your part. There are several reasons for this.

As individuals, we can tend to be self-deprecating. We underestimate our skills, and we think, "If I can do it, anyone can." There is a built-in tendency toward unpretentiousness and believing others are equally as skilled as we are in any given area. Humility can be a virtue, but a continual self-deprecating mindset that devalues our personal strengths is a detriment to our prosperity and success.

There are skills that you possess and operate at a higher level more than those around you. As you chart your course to a fulfilling and prosperous life, you will recognize areas of strength among your personal traits and recognize that you have the ability to become extraordinary. Sometimes it helps if you realize that you are not prideful, but you are accepting the gifts that God gave you. I have used the question "what can you become the best in the world at" in executive coaching exercises.

Many people fail to identify their own areas of extraordinary skill where they have the potential for greatness because they operate in those areas naturally, with little effort, and wonder why others are struggling. They are dumbfounded when someone else can't see it because the solution is so apparent to them or the physical task is so easy for them.

INTENSE PRACTICE: THE 10,000-HOUR RULE

Malcolm Gladwell in his book *Outliers: The Story of Success* popularized a scientific finding by researchers who discovered that those who become the world's master craftsmen spend a minimum of 10,000 hours in training and practice of their skill. That is the equivalent of ten years of preparation at about 20 hours per week.

Gladwell outlines the stories of the Beatles and Microsoft as examples. In both instances, he argues their world-class success was not due to chance, but development of skills. They identified, honed, and practiced for 10,000 hours the thing they could be best in the world at.

SKILL AND TIME MANAGEMENT

One foundation in fulfilling 10,000 hours of practice needed for mastery as defined by Gladwell is skillful management of your time. For the past 20 years, I have led many seminars and workshops on the topic of time management. Because of the importance of the time necessary to develop true expertise, successful individuals are those who have significant time mastery skills.

At different levels, we often have too much to do and not enough time to accomplish it. In order to continually develop our skills, we have to make tough choices. Time is inflexible; therefore, we must adapt and employ self-management and discipline if we are to possess expertise in any skill.

High-in-demand experts have "paid the price" by continually choosing skill development activities like studying, reading, practicing, and training over other less important activities competing for their time. Simply put, those things of highest value to us must be scheduled in priority to ensure they are accomplished. If this is not the case, those things of lesser importance will fill our schedule and keep us from full development of important areas of life.

"PRACTICE IS THE CAUSE OF ACHIEVEMENT"

Daniel J. Levitin, author of *This Is Your Brain on Music: The Science of a Human Obsession*. Levitin is a neuroscientist and psychology professor at McGill University in Montreal. He wrote that time spent in practicing a skill is the most important factor in determining success. Practice provides a level playing field where people of many backgrounds and talents can achieve greatness.

> In several studies, the very best conservatory students were found to have practiced the most, sometimes twice as much as those who weren't judged as good....In another study... several years later, the students who achieved the highest performance

ratings were those who had practiced the most, irrespective of which "talent" group they had been assigned to previously. This suggests that practice is the cause of achievement, not merely something correlated with it.

MASTERY

Those who develop their skills in that private world of personal practice gain the ability to be in demand in their field. In every aspect of life, skills can make the difference in how much impact you have on others. No amount of expertise in the Circles of Spirit or Self-Mastery can compensate for lack of or poor performing skills.

When you achieve mastery in a skill set, you are not only highly capable, but also known for being innovative and possessing emotional strength, creativity, and extreme focus.

ROLE OF MENTAL ATTITUDE IN DEVELOPING SKILLS

Two waiters were scheduled to work on the same day at a certain restaurant. When one woke up, a familiar thought pattern from childhood filled his mind with resentment of abusive situations from the past, failure in college, and perceived mistreatment by almost everyone, including his current employer. He dressed carelessly for work, and he was not attentive to the patrons he was serving. His untidy clothes and his attitude revealed the inner condition of his interior thoughts.

His coworker awoke with an entirely different mindset. He was full of gratitude as he prepared for work, because he had been studying college courses online and he saw his job as a means to continue his education. As a waiter, he had met some incredible people through interactions on the job. He was intentional about looking for opportunities to learn from those he encountered. These new people had given him critical information that had helped him shape his education and his life plan. Restaurant work was hard, but it helped instill in him a sense of exactitude and excellence that he could transfer to other jobs.

Here's my question. At the end of the night, whose pockets do you think would be filled with tips? I'm sure you'll agree it's the man with the self-empowering thought pattern and lifestyle. He was mentally focused on his life plan and daily taking steps to achieve it.

The first waiter was focused on his problems. He had not matured to the point in life where we mentally switch from focusing on our problems and weaknesses to evaluating and capitalizing on our strengths. For most of us, this takes place subtly and naturally as we move forward into careers, vocations, and avocations.

We all must transition from focusing on our disadvantages, shortcomings, weaknesses, and undeveloped areas to focusing on our strengths and corresponding skill development. It is largely a personal decision and a function of individual intentionality.

> Taking initiative, coupled with focused action, is at the heart of the needed skill of proactivity.

THE SKILL OF PROACTIVITY

Taking initiative, coupled with focused action, is at the heart of the needed skill of proactivity. Stephen Covey wrote about proactivity in his book, *The 7 Habits of Highly Effective People: Powerful Lessons in Personal Change,* in the context of taking responsibility for the direction of your life. This includes not only what you do, but also what you think. A profound change happens when we realize our life is not at the mercy of external variables. Each of us has the ability to choose, even in situations where our choices can be limited; we ultimately have the ability to choose how we view those situations.

Proactivity is self-initiated behavior that results in forward action. It is based on your realization that you are ultimately in charge of what you choose to do or not to do. Actions taken in alignment with your passion cause you to chart your course and own your life. Proactivity is taking control of your life plan and making things happen for your own advancement, rather than waiting for somebody else to make it happen. My observation is that individuals can take years waiting to be discovered while they should have been taking initiative. To say it clearly, only you can help you. This can only be done by taking responsibility for your thoughts and actions and being proactive.

REJECTING NEGATIVE THINKING

Precious time is wasted every day on self-defeating thoughts and blame-filled thinking that could have been employed in skill development. As you embark on significant life changes, you may be battered by negative thoughts, past failures, and the criticism of others. If left unchecked, these thoughts can keep you from the ultimate goal of proactively taking control and responsibility for your life decisions. Rejecting negative thinking is a skill.

Here are examples of negative thoughts that hinder proactivity and progress which should be rejected:

She makes me angry.

I'm just like my father.

It's just not in the cards for me.

I'm not old enough.

I'm too old.

Proactive thinking—She can't make me angry; it's always my choice on how I will respond. It's me. I won't blame others any more. I have seen people realize with a jolt that they have been placing blame on others. This, in turn, relinquishes personal control by ascribing the power of change to others. "*If she would only stop _____, then I could _____.*" One of the most freeing realizations comes when we understand that despite the actions of others, I alone have the ability to choose how I will act and respond.

Negative thinking—It's not me. If only you would change. Not wanting to accept responsibility, individuals want to continue placing blame on others. Often, these mental crutches have been in place for so long that to remove them by taking responsibility would mean notable change in their conversation, attitude, and actions.

OVERCOMING OBSTACLES

I have learned that individuals from dismal and dysfunctional backgrounds have a strong, pervasive temptation to hold disempowering views of the future based on their history. Old negative voices and past experiences have a way of projecting themselves into their future.

I've always been this way.

Nothing works out for me.

I'm setting myself up for disappointment. I'm going to quit now.

My father always told me I would never amount to anything.

You are not destined to be a product of your past! You have a unique ability and responsibility to place empowering interpretations on your past. Further connecting with God (through the activities outlined in the Spirit Circle) gives you the infinite ability to recreate yourself anew. This process begins with taking proactive control of every mindset in life.

SKILL OF REACTING TO REJECTION

Learning how to deal with rejection and criticism is a life skill that, when mastered, will help you unlock many others. Let's say an individual is unduly criticized or rejected at their workplace. Fear, defeatism, self-pity, and resignation based on faulty self-talk can develop into disempowering mindsets.

My ideas are never good enough.

I never get the recognition I deserve.

The boss has favorites.

I'm afraid of losing my job.

Many individuals never take advantage of the opportunity to develop the skill to handle rejection and develop empowering self-talk.

SELF-EMPOWERING DURING TIMES OF SETBACK

Realistically, there will always be criticisms and temporary setbacks as we hone our skills. However, you can choose to view them as challenges. This is a powerful and productive truth.

Do not take too lightly the need to regulate your internal conversations during situations of seeming setback. The difference between ultimate success and failure often lies in your ability to reframe your internal conversation and employ self-empowering thoughts.

We have all seen how two people can have the same experience, yet one of them tells the story with an empowering view of how much she learned and accomplished while the other one tells the same story with despair, anger, and a sense of fatalism.

I have a lifestyle where I'm engaged often in public speaking, sometimes to large audiences. Often, right before stepping up onto the platform to speak, some event or conversation will occur that could cause a stream of debilitating thoughts. Someone might suggest that the conference attendance is low or I might hear a negative comment about another speaker—these potentially negative comments are often amplified by the common anxiety around performing well as a public speaker. I've found that it's necessary for me to sequester myself into an environment, physically or just mentally, where I can take the time to remember and review the hundreds of encouraging comments from people who have benefited from my books and events. It's important to recall why you are doing what you are doing and gain the positive thoughts that will work to empower you.

FULFILLING YOUR POTENTIAL

If you ever get tired of going through life frustrated from fighting lifelong currents that go against your unique gifts, leaving them untapped and undefined, you can change.

You may know someone who has had vast training in a field but after talking with them, you discover that something is not lining up between who they are and what they are doing. A nurse is missing the deep compassion and patience necessary for that vocation. A friend you see every day has the potential for greatness but never musters the boldness needed to pursue their dreams.

If you were to take the time to analyze each person's story, you would find that many of these people never embarked on the journey to become congruent with their true selves. Many think it's too late to develop new skill sets aligned with their unique passions. For example, if they are in a hard-driving sales environment, but they have a passion for creativity, they can live in a constant state of frustration.

Imagine that a man or woman loves accounting for every last dollar. This awakens something within them, and they find meaning and purpose in this task. If that person works in an environment that is solely based on human interaction and a zest for people skills, they would probably live a life of frustration.

You are not too old or too advanced in your career or your life to embark on this change in your journey. I have seen transformative times of change, that should have taken years, be fulfilled in a matter of weeks. All it often takes is the courage to start.

Often the smallest of changes and intentional movement toward planning your passion, charting your course, and owning your life can yield substantial results. In chemistry, if you change one chemical in a chemical compound, you change the entire substance. Likewise, changing one component of your life to become congruent with who you are and what matters most causes a chain reaction that begins to unleash your hidden potential.

You have a unique mandate to fulfill. This journey might seem overwhelming if you looked at all the steps to be accomplished, so focus on the first few.

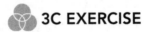 3C EXERCISE

Set up the 3C Skill Plan and charting your course, and owning your life by identifying and initiating action. Use *The 3C Companion Guide* to record your responses to these topics to maximize and deploy your greatest strengths.

Consider your skills in these areas:

- What skills are unique to you?

- What can you be the best in the world at?

- Can you develop a simple and consistent plan for personal skill development?

- What skills do you see as gifts from God?

- What skills give you a competitive advantage?

- What skills would you enjoy developing?

- What skills and activities are needed to fulfill your life plan?

CHAPTER 6

CIRCLE OF SELF-MASTERY

"He opened the big box, and Dorothy saw that it was filled with spectacles of every size and shape. All of them had green glasses in them. The Guardian of the Gates found a pair that would just fit Dorothy and put them over her eyes. There were two golden bands fastened to them that passed around the back of her head, where they were locked together by a little key that was at the end of a chain the Guardian of the Gates wore around his neck."

—*THE WONDERFUL WIZARD OF OZ* by L. Frank (Lyman Frank) Baum[1]

One iconic moment in motion picture history is the unmasking of the all-powerful, all-knowing Wizard of Oz in front of the cowering quartet of Dorothy, the Tin Man, the Cowardly Lion, and the Scarecrow. As they bow before a flashing image of the Wizard, seeking his help, the facade of the smoke and mirrors is overwhelming until the little dog Toto pulls back the curtain. Suddenly, they discover that it is all an illusion. The "Great Wizard" is actually a feeble old man working his sound system, images, and pulleys from behind a curtain. Oz had created this persona that he wanted others to see, instead of seeing who he really was.

In the original book called *The Wonderful Wizard of Oz* by L. Frank Baum, before Dorothy and the others meet the Wizard, they arrive at the gate of the Emerald City where each one is fitted with a pair of green-tinted glasses before they are allowed to enter. The tinted glasses give every resident and visitor the illusion that the city is built from green emeralds.

PERSONAS AND PERSONAL BIASES

Just like the Wizard of Oz, all of us have a lens we use to view ourselves and our world. This lens can often be distorted. We also each have a persona of how we would like the world to view us, and often it is not a real depiction of who we are or how we're perceived. We often feel the need to present a better version of ourselves. This persona becomes a way to filter how we interact with the world around us and, at its core, it hinders us from maturing and growing in Self-Mastery.

Also, just like those tinted glasses in Oz, we all go through life with our own tinted view of the world that we have formed from our personal likes and dislikes, propensities, and habits. This process begins during our early years. The distortions from our personal biases and prejudices can become extreme, as in the case of phobias, violent prejudice, hatred, or unsettling fears. They can also be benign and manifested in preferences for jobs, employees, friends, likes and dislikes that each of us possesses.

Each of us, regardless of education, background, study, and culture, has been fitted with a pair of glasses. The question is not *if* you will develop colored lenses to view the world, but whether you are willing to admit on a day-to-day basis that you are using them (your personal biases) to make decisions and to form opinions. In self-mastery, it is important that we can let the world see who we truly are and also take a clear undistorted look at individuals and the world around us.

PERSONAL GROWTH IN SELF-MASTERY

When I examine the lives and personalities of prosperous people who have achieved a high level of Spirit, Skills, and Self-Mastery, their self-worth and purpose allow them the freedom to be themselves and to constantly develop in maturity. They have strong character qualities and a commitment to the underlying principles of fulfilment and prosperity.

Four Levels of Self-Mastery

There are four classic progressive levels of Self-Mastery. These four levels will give you a grid for gauging your own personal growth and experience.

Once you can identify where you are and understand areas of needed transformation, you can begin to grow in your unique 3C Self-Mastery Circle.

Self-Mastery Overview

Level 1—Self-Awareness. Like the people of Oz, at first you don't know that you are wearing green glasses and you think that what you see is the only reality. Self-awareness is a mirror stage where you begin to see yourself more accurately. This process takes honest reflection, self-examination, and some courage. You become aware of your green glasses—your private, often inaccurate, interpretation of everything in the world—so that you can begin to see the need to adjust to reality and begin the process of Self-Management.

Level 2—Self-Management. You begin changing the needed areas of your life using focused awareness and by applying personal discipline. You put aside any persona allowing for increased congruency and openness. Self-Management is the lifelong process of true self-identification coupled with practical self-change. You identify things about yourself that need to be improved, and you courageously confront and begin to change them.

Level 3—Empathy. You have made so much progress in Self-Awareness and Self-Mastery that you are now able to consistently look beyond your own needs and tinted vision to understand others. You develop a true desire to recognize others, even with opposing views, without judgment. You develop "positive regard,"[2] which accepts and supports a person notwithstanding what they say or do. The term is believed to have been coined by the psychologist Carl Rogers. It involves valuing and recognizing the best in people and the world around you. At this level, you are now affirming others and their potential, while engaging in exploration, discovery, and the search for the best in people.

Empathy entails understanding, not necessarily agreement.

You can now work effectively with a team. You may also be entrusted with greater responsibilities under authority. People begin to be drawn to you naturally.

Level 4—Leadership. At this stage, you are an empathetic and objective facilitator of change. You can discern when to help others and when to stand back and let them solve problems on their own, so that they can grow. You embody the qualities of fairness and inspiration. You have high expectations, but provide encouragement, support, and recognition. As you move beyond your own self-interest, you inspire others to do the same. You can be trusted with high levels of leadership and are considered a statesman in the way you carry yourself.

SELF-MASTERY LEVEL 1— SELF-AWARENESS

Lack of Self-Awareness

It has been my experience that many individuals cause themselves and those around them a great deal of pain and abrasion when they lack Self-Awareness. They are not aware that their view of the world is simply their own personal perspective. There is an overwhelming need to force their views and opinions on others. It's their individual worldview and it has a tinted lens. This view is colored by prejudices, background experiences, education, inner wounding, and cultural perspectives.

When they interact with others, they do not recognize that they have biases, so they are continually confronting people and being confronted themselves. They find it difficult, if not impossible, to see the viewpoints of others or admit when they are wrong. This becomes a never-ending, awkward way of finding their way among those with differing opinions, mindsets, backgrounds, and worldviews.

Their emotional outbursts can continue unbridled. They seldom become aware of the damage caused by escalated emotion.

Without Self-Awareness, you are not aware of your limitations or how you're perceived by the world around you. You are uninformed and underexposed. You don't know what you don't know.

Before Self-Awareness, you are mostly self-centered and biased, and this is obvious to others. However, through Self-Awareness you become aware that you have not been objective about how you have viewed the affairs of life. You have seen everything your own way. You thought your view was the only infallible view of the world. When you woke up and realized that you were wearing green glasses, you took them off.

Thinking back on people and situations, I'm sure you would be able to more easily identify people who had different levels of success in many arenas, but were defeated in the area of Self-Awareness. They were like bulls in a china shop—trampling on people, their ideas, and their perspectives. They either seem victimized or tyrannical. They were unable to be proactive because they were putting the blame on others around them whom they feel simply "don't get it." Meanwhile, they lack the ability and the skill necessary for Self-Awareness.

Self-Awareness is the foundation of Emotional Intelligence.[3] It is the ability to view yourself interacting in a situation objectively to see how you look to others.

It is an important step in the process of Self-Mastery.

Need for Self-Awareness

The need for Self-Awareness is becoming more and more crucial as our planet becomes more globalized. Every day, we find ourselves interacting with people with significantly different cultures, upbringings, backgrounds, religions, ideals, likes, and dislikes.

Cultural biases are perhaps the deepest level where we need to reorient our lenses. Our lenses have been crafted at a young age with literally thousands of cultural preferences of which most of us remain unaware. Cultural differences are so pervasive that we receive impressions from parents, teachers, co-workers, television, films, billboards, advertising, and other means in both overt and covert ways.

In the early stages of building Self-Awareness, there may be a somewhat negative connotation to the process because you are being awakened to a true view of self with all of your faults as well as your abilities.

ENGAGING THE RIGHT FRIENDS TO ADVISE YOU

Example Conversation

I have often used third-party objectivity to aid me in my interactions. This can provide the needed perspective to vastly increase Self-Awareness. Here is an example that you can adopt and use. John says, "Fred, I'm going to take a chance to talk with Bill today about collaborating on some projects. Tell me what you think about this conversation."

Then John begins to role-play a possible conversation as Fred listens. John has taken a step toward Self-Mastery by proactively seeking Fred's third-party objectivity. This will help him to compensate for his own blind spots and the limitations of the lens with which he views the world.

Fred responds, "John, that sounds great, but you might be a little too strident in a couple of areas that Bill might interpret as being overly assertive. I think a few changes in your phraseology will build more consensus."

John will likely be spared now from a negative reaction by Bill that could have derailed the project.

Open Interaction

The power of taking a few simple steps that open us up to honest communication is a profound advantage in every area of our lives—from interaction with our children to interaction on business or social levels, from public speaking to inter-personal communication. The key is gaining Self-Awareness—the ability to come outside of your personal perspective and view a conversation or setting with third-party objectivity.

SELF-MASTERY LEVEL 2— SELF-MANAGEMENT

Self-*Awareness* is the Level of Self-Mastery where you learn to see yourself as you truly are, with all your positive and negative tendencies. Self-*Management* is Level 2 of Self-Mastery where you move from observations about yourself to actively changing yourself.

Self-Management of Emotions

Certain levels of anger, frustration, or anxiety can cause you to lose your objectivity and blind your Self-Awareness. Physiologically, chemicals are released into your bloodstream that further distort your perspective. You become too insistent on making your point and could care less about how you are coming across.

Try to recognize early signs that your emotions may be becoming problematic before they become chemically enhanced, because once they reach this level, it will take time for your body to dissipate these effects. If you think you may be overreacting, stand up and take a break. It's important for each of us to know ourselves well enough that when we are getting into a situation of heightened emotions, we learn how to recognize it and how to take action to compensate.

SELF-MASTERY LEVEL 3— EMPATHY

Living a life of empathy opens the door to vast and profound levels of interpersonal interaction. Empathy is not sympathy. Sympathy is a sense of emotional pity for a person who has a different view, situation, or station in life. You give sympathy based on a value judgment of another person's life. You feel sorry for them, mostly because they are not like you.

Empathy is uniquely different in that it employs the art of understanding. To be empathic is to probe more deeply into a situation, trying to understand an individual's unique perspective. When you are empathetic, you try to look though other people's eyes and take on their viewpoint without judging. In short, you walk in their shoes and use their lenses to view a situation from their perspective.

Empathy touches a basic human need in others to feel understood and valued. It is difficult, if not impossible, to move on to higher levels of engagement with someone unless that individual feels respected. An empathetic mindset can produce some of life's most positive transformative experiences, especially when others are diametrically opposed to you at first. You're able to see interactions change as others sense your nonjudgmental desire to understand them.

Surprised by Empathy

Some time ago, I was scheduled for an appointment with a banking executive at my office, but while he was waiting for me I became tied up in traffic. While the staff of our pharmaceutical and hotel accounting office tried to cover for me, he noticed on my desk boxes of literature about our humanitarian response to a recent famine in East Africa. He began to read the literature that described the crisis of recently orphaned children and our relief efforts that were underway among companies I had started.

Most individuals feel sorry for and are sympathetic to this type of story, but sympathy can cause short superficial reaction. For the banking executive that read through this material while waiting for me to arrive, he was moved to empathy from the stories he was reading. By the time I made it to the office, the executive had tears in his eyes and his personal checkbook in hand. He became a most unlikely but most welcome corporate donor. As a by-product, our relationship changed. He saw me and my corporate endeavors from a new perspective. From that point on, we became friends.

Religion and Empathy

Many religious individuals find empathy difficult. In my experience, religious leaders can lack this needed skill because their desire to make their views known is so pronounced that they have difficulty allowing others enough mental space to feel accepted and valued. This happens more frequently if the individuals have dramatically opposing views to their religious beliefs. The religious leader can feel that they are condoning others behavior and lifestyle if they were to ask questions to gain clarity.

> Once you can understand and manage yourself and empathize or understand others' viewpoints, then you can begin to effectively compel and lead others to action.

SELF-MASTERY LEVEL 4— LEADERSHIP

The fourth level of Self-Mastery is Leadership or managing others. This can be family leadership, corporate leadership, or community leadership. Whatever type of leadership, it builds from our developed place of Self-Awareness, Self-Mastery, and Empathy. Once you can understand and manage yourself and empathize or understand others' viewpoints, then you can begin to effectively compel and lead others to action. You become a facilitator of change.

There are volumes written on leadership, its components, and practices, but for our purposes we will contain our view of leadership in light of advanced Self-Mastery. Some of you reading this might say that you are not in a position of leadership. I would argue each of us has leadership roles. You may be a homemaker, or a father, or involved in a civic organization; I assure you, there are those around you who you can impact through leadership.

Leadership is the result of a lifelong endeavor that begins with self-evaluation, empathy, and the realization that each person's unique perspectives are just that—uniquely individual. At the heart of this approach is setting an example that inspires others to follow. Without this, many unconsciously say "do as I say, not as I do." This is especially evident when we attempt to lead those closest to us, family, friends, and others with personal relationship. At this level, without Self-Awareness and Self-Management, others can spot hypocrisy and incongruence between what we teach and how we live. How many parents have felt this sting as children model their actions more than obey their directives?

HELP YOURSELF FIRST

Recently, while I was traveling on a plane, the stewardess said, "If you are traveling with a child or someone who needs assistance, put on your oxygen mask first so that you will be able to help others around you." It occurred to me that this principle applies to many facets of life. It is important for us to engage in personal self-development and self-mastery so that we will be able to contribute on an ongoing, significant basis to the world around us.

 3C EXERCISE

- Have you been able to recognize personal biases?

- How does this aid you in your personal growth in Self-Mastery?

- In varying degrees within different aspects of our lives we can be at diverse stages of the Four Levels of Self-Mastery. Honestly take time to assess your competence in the following areas:
  - Level 1—Self-Awareness
  - Level 2—Self-Management

- Level 3—Empathy
- Level 4—Leadership

- How can you employ the strategy "Help Yourself First" as it applies to life?

The *3C Companion Guide* has expanded and corresponding questions designed to give you further thought and application.

ENDNOTES

1. L. Frank (Lyman Frank) Baum, *The Wonderful Wizard of Oz*. Chicago: April, 1900 (Kindle Edition in the Public Domain).

2. Carl Rogers, *A Way of Being* (1900).

3. See also Chapter 3, "Before We Begin, Emotional Alignment."

CHAPTER 7

KEYS TO MAINTAINING A FULFILLING AND PROSPEROUS FUTURE

"You can chain me, you can torture me, you can even destroy this body, but you will never imprison my mind."
—MAHATMA GANDHI

The last section of this book is vital and devoted to practical application and keys to deploying your personal 3C Strategy toward planning your passion, charting your course, and owning your life. This entails developing a sustainable 3C root system. What does it mean to be rooted and grounded in a "core system" that is empowering and promoting a fulfilling successful life? This occurs when your deepest underlying beliefs are supporting you and nourishing you—your beliefs help you with every step toward fulfilment and prosperity. When you are firmly rooted in a positive 3C belief system, your default mindset is one that continuously supports your progress.

Roots represent that place in your life that others can't see. They contain intentional times alone where we self-examine and strengthen our core beliefs, dreams, and attitudes. Just as roots dig into the soil for both nourishment and supportive strength, the time we spend envisioning and planning our fulfilling and prosperous life provide the mental and emotional foundation "roots" we need. Someone once said, "the fruit we see is the result of roots we cannot."

CORE VALUES

You will need to identify both your current core values as well as those you must develop, in order to see lasting change occur in your life. In my experience, uncovering these core values is one of the most significant and profound journeys of discovery a person can take in their lifetime. A person cannot find true direction without knowing their core values. Core values are like the operating system of a computer that allows other applications to run smoothly.

RECOGNIZING SELF-DEFEAT IS A KEY TO HAVING A FULFILLING AND PROSPEROUS MINDSET

To draw a comparison between a healthy and an unhealthy root system, let's juxtapose the major core values prized by dysfunctional subcultures. They have a quest for the ability to never be taken advantage of. You'll find conversational statements like:

No one is going to pull anything over on me.

I saw that one coming.

Everyone has an angle.

She is a fool for being so generous.

No one can be fully trusted.

There is a deep cynicism toward people and life in general. Negativity abounds in their conversations and their evaluations of others. Even if someone comes to them with the purest of motives or opportunities, they always respond with suspicion and contempt.

Are you influenced by a cynical mentality? Have you been influenced by a worldview with ideologies such as:

- Never let anyone take advantage of you.
- Everyone has an angle, and they are always trying to take advantage of you.
- There are not enough resources to go around, so you better get yours first.
- I'll take from you before I go without.
- I am always suspicious of everyone and their motivations.

These thought patterns have been dramatically influential in the formation of the worldview and paradigms of many. If unchecked, they continue to run in the background and hinder us from moving forward to plan our passion and chart our course to a fulfilling and prosperous life.

Over the years of working with hundreds of CEOs and high-impact individuals, I have come to believe that the concept you are about to learn is a foundational theme in the lives of most of the prosperous individuals I have met.

PLANNED INNOCENCE

Most of us have been brought up in an environment where we have been trained to spot flaws and errors. We have been trained to look for trouble.

However, with self-determination and practice, we can constantly refresh our mental attitudes after daily disappointments and return to what I have termed "planned innocence." Even when things go wrong, we can train ourselves to mentally reestablish a mindset of faith in other people and hope in the world around us. It's important, because otherwise we shut ourselves off from possible relationships and opportunities, too busy protecting ourselves to realize that we are missing out on life.

When you are a trusting person, you are able to focus on the good in people, not their faults. A lifetime of *planned innocence* plays out in the lives of people who have gained great impact, significance, and prosperity.

Often there is a balance to be struck. If you consider a range on a continuum, cynicism would be on one side and gullibility would be on the other side. Different situations can require adjusting on this continuum. The intentional practice of *planned innocence* helps you to continuously come back to a state of trust and openness, while still being mindful that we live in an imperfect world.

ENLISTING THE HELP OF OTHERS AS YOU CHART YOUR COURSE

A quick note about trusting and informing others concerning your personal goals and progress. Your close relationships and friendships can help or hinder you on your road to accomplishing your goal of a fulfilling and prosperous life. I'm sure you have learned this already, but here is a powerful key that can help.

If there is something you are trying to quit, such as smoking, overeating etc., as a general rule, you should tell all your close relationships. Their continual accountability will be very helpful to keep you in check. "Why are you eating that cake? You said you were on a diet."

If you have aspirations that transcend your present levels of accomplishment, these goals should be shared discreetly and only in close relationships where the other person truly desires to see you succeed. Sadly, jealousy, insecurity, and misunderstanding can often cause people to react negatively or worse impede your progress.

Further, keeping your goals private often supports accomplishment. Your good feelings from sharing your goals may prematurely satisfy you and you stop working. Derek Sivers, founder of CD Baby, believes it is better to keep some goals secret. Our minds sometimes associate fulfilment of goals with the simple step of sharing it with others.

Honestly ask yourself, during challenging times has your internal thought process been one of empowerment or have you noticed cynicism rising? How do you think this affected the outcome of these challenging moments?

When you examine these questions and adjust your responses, you can develop a root system that enables you to consistently chart your course to a fulfilling and prosperous life.

 **3C EXERCISE**

Recognizing self-defeat is a key to having a fulfilling and prosperous mindset. Often there is a balance to be struck. If you consider a range on a continuum, cynicism would be on one side and gullibility would be on the other side.

- What has been your natural tendency on the continuum of cynicism and gullibility?

- With regard to a prosperous mindset, what are your unique

keys to maintaining a fulfilling and prosperous future?

- Can your mindset toward others be changed to help you to be more effective?

- Have you been wise in enlisting the help of others as you chart your course?

CHAPTER 8

LOVE YOUR LIFE AND LEARN FROM YOUR SETBACKS

"Most great people have attained their greatest success just one step beyond their greatest failure."
—NAPOLEON HILL

SETBACK STRATEGIES: RECOVERY AND AVOIDANCE

Adversity and obstacles will come to all lives at one time or another to varying degrees. Sometimes, obstacles that seem insurmountable block your way. By programming yourself to see them as challenges and stepping stones to success, you will be able to keep yourself free from the swamp of disillusion, depression, and despair.

> The most important conversation of your life—the one you have with yourself.

As we discussed earlier, your internal thought life moves at an astounding rate of 600–700 words per minute. It is your job to be rigorous in your effort to control the most important conversation of your life—the one you have with yourself. Begin by simply using different language. Instead of saying "I have a problem," you could restate it as "I have a personal challenge" or "There are some obstacles to be overcome." Changing your vocabulary creates a significant adjustment in your thought life.

I have come to believe that God has given each of us the power of choice and one important choice is how to view moments of defeat.

Recovery. Throughout history, we can look at extreme cases of individuals who have gone to the depths of ruin and poverty only to recover at their lowest point and become prolific role models of reaching one's potential. These have become a source of inspiration for those of us who have grown up in environments that did not provide all the opportunities we would have liked. Their lives inspire many who have suffered extreme setbacks and come to their lowest point, being perceived as failures by others. Many of these setbacks were unavoidable.

> How we view the process of recovery when we experience temporary setbacks can make the difference between being stuck and enjoying continuous advancement.

Avoidance. However, there are also numerous stories of individuals who were able to avoid setbacks by studying the lives of others and learning from them. It's a common story—the dramatic recovery from bankruptcy or overcoming hardships. These are usually inspirational stories, but the less-dramatic story of avoiding bankruptcy often remains unnoticed, but is equally motivating.

Part of the human condition is suffering setbacks. Regardless of the cause, the pain and ripple effect from these setbacks can be absolutely overwhelming unless you decide in advance that you will continue to love your life and you will learn something new from every setback that comes your way. This advanced preparation allows you to dust yourself off and move ahead without missing a stride.

Let's look at an example. Someone might wake up, get ready for work, and when they step outside, they find they've got a flat tire while their car was sitting in the driveway. One type of person would say, "God hates me. I'm already having such a bad day. I'm going to be so late to work that I'm going to get fired."

Another person with the same situation would look at the tire and say, "This is so fortunate that it happened right here where

I can get it fixed. I could have been on the highway last night when it was raining and I was with my family! Everyone has a flat tire once in a while. I'm sure my boss will understand. Maybe I'll meet someone at the repair shop today who will be a good contact for me."

It's the same event—the same flat tire but the response can be completely different.

3C EXERCISE

- In the past have you been able to love your life and learn from your setbacks?

- What have been you views on Recovery and Avoidance?

- What has been your experience with the most important conversation of your life—the one you have with yourself?

Has it been empowering? How can you change to make improvements?

- Consider a time in your past of a specific setback. After having gained time and perspective, how can you see the situation differently? As you consider this situation, how did your perspective change and what did you learn that you can apply to similar obstacles in the future?

- Consider your life as a timeline that maps out the high and low points but has a continuing upward moving trend. Think of ways you can use this perspective when you are met with short-term challenges and obstacles.

Use these questions to help you gain your own third-party perspective and begin seeing your setbacks in a positive light. Use the *3C Companion Guide* to record your responses to these and further questions.

CHAPTER 9

PROACTIVE VISUALIZATION

"I skate to where the puck is going to be, not where it has been."
—WAYNE GRETZKY,
Retired as leading point scorer in
National Hockey League history

POSITIVE MENTAL VISUALIZATION BY OLYMPIC ATHLETES

All of us have started strong on some new diet, exercise routine, or project, or turned over a new leaf in the proverbial New Year's resolutions only to leave them behind a short while later. We have bought new treadmills, bikes, exercise equipment, that after a few months have become excellent coatracks pushed into the corner.

In my early years, I must admit that was my pattern. It was often difficult for me to stay focused on any new strategy. I found mental training makes the difference between success and failure, so we must learn to engage in this process. This essential key has been well documented in many areas.

In one of the most well-known studies on visualization, Russian scientists compared three groups of Olympic athletes, rating their physical and mental visualization ratios.

- *Group 1* received 100 percent physical training.

- *Group 2* received 75 percent physical training with 25 percent mental training.

- *Group 3* received 50 percent mental training with 50 percent physical training.

Remarkably, Group 3 had the best performance results. Similar studies validate that mental training has significant, measurable effects on lasting performance. Engaging active mental training, or in some of us retraining, involves the focused visualization and mental reinforcement of our intended goals.

Similarly, the past decade has seen a marked increase in the number of companies and executives who are hiring executive coaches.

However, these sessions may produce only *short-term gains*—a honeymoon effect— in many cases, unfortunately, the initial impact quickly wanes. At first, there seems to come a leveling up. Then there is a return to former levels or even lower.

To accomplish lasting change, the best executive coaching delivers permanent changes in deeper areas such as perceptions, lifestyles, and culture of the company.

I've come to believe that one of the most profound core skills necessary to uncap the hidden wealth within, to release the treasure and destiny of our lives, is to recognize and eliminate internal saboteurs that continually defeat us. There are many internal factors that cause us to give up before we start. Almost always they are rooted in our subconscious. Take the steps to become a champion over your thought life and you will be effective and prosperous on a consistent basis.

POSITIVE VISUALIZATION

Start to visualize yourself in new settings related to your future prosperity. Then you can begin to get a picture of how your future self will look in order to be congruent with those surroundings. This small exercise can help you to see your future self in order to live in this new environment.

Visualize the person you want to be, what your relationships will look like, who you are, the types of endeavors you are embarking on, and how you are responding and interacting in these settings. Become rooted in "why" this new life is important. Mentally envision the related benefits of this new life and how this will help others around you.

Someone once profoundly stated, "No matter where you go, there you are." If we continually find ourselves in turmoil and friction among differing groups and environments, we ourselves can be the common denominator. At a deeper level, each of us has the ability and the responsibility to change ourselves. Often in doing this internally, our external environment responds.

MENTAL DIET

For years, psychologists have tried to analyze where thoughts come from—what is their inception. The old adage "you are what you eat" cannot be more true when it comes to our mental diet. Therefore, you need to redirect your thought life to something significantly positive. When you focus on fulfilling a personal life plan that is supported by your own belief in that life plan, then your mind will stay occupied and progress is assured.

When you talk with people who are not deliberate about fulfilling their destiny, they may be passionate about generic goals. "I want to make money. I want to do this and that and make things happen."

However, when you ask, "What is your *personal* plan? Where are *you* going? What are *you* doing to fulfill *your* destiny?" they don't have a plan. And because they don't, they can't visualize their future clearly.

Initially, developing a life plan and creatively visualizing it may seem somewhat ethereal or hard to grasp. As you begin this process, it will become more clear, like focusing a camera lens.

SELF-PREOCCUPATION

I want to say at the outset of this process that I'm not a fan of continuous psychological self-evaluation. Internal psychological analysis is not what I'm advocating. This can lead to what I have called "Self-Preoccupation" where too much time is spent in self-focus and analysis. It has been my experience that prolonged self-analysis and other forms of critical introspection not only fails to produce the type of change we would like to see, but can lead us into a swamp, a downward spiral of psychological introspection. If you continually look for flaws in yourself, your past, or others, you're sure to find them.

A proactive, positive self-evaluation will draw out from you the type of person that you should be visualizing. This method of self-evaluation is geared to unearth those thoughts that are congruent with your own unique life direction and core purposes.

Your goal is not to discover how you have missed the mark or continually dredge up past pain. You seek to discover those characteristics to develop in your personality to prepare for the future, those internal treasures that make you unique among all people.

Once you define through self-discovery who you are and where you are going, you can build upon that strong foundation structures that will last.

PROACTIVE EVALUATION

Let's look at this from another standpoint. If you live a life that is not proactive, without positive visualization, then you are living in a constant reactive state. This life is not based on planning your passion or charting your course and owning your life, but instead it's based on responding to other people's demands and expectations and the busyness and distraction of life. If you never take that time to clearly visualize the future prosperity and life that you want to obtain, then you cannot reach the congruency needed between that picture and the process of maturity in order to make that picture a reality. Make the choice today.

> If you never take the time to visualize the life that you want to obtain, then you cannot reach the congruency between that picture and the process of maturity to make that picture a reality.

SETTING GOALS BASED ON YOUR 3C STRATEGY

No matter how hard you try or how great your attitude, you will never get anywhere using the wrong map. Life goals are unique to each person, and though there may be some similarities, you cannot follow another person's plan as if their life map is identical to yours. If you try to apply the methods, systems, and tactics someone else has used to reach their personal goals and destinations in life, you will be disappointed. Your life is just too unique and personalized to do this.

UNIQUE GOALS

The diet guru, the self-help coach, and the business mogul who offer concrete steps to success in their realm of influence are vastly different from you. They have different body types, different upbringings, metabolisms, educations, and resources. In fact, the differences are infinite. They can be well-meaning and successful in their own individualized journey, but you can actually find yourself using the wrong map by trying to mimic them.

Whether in the realm of diet, finance, business development, or personal actualization, it is vital to understand that you cannot simply mimic the systems and methods of others. You must develop those that are unique and take into consideration your unique state.

Instead of looking for a detailed life plan from someone else, do the work yourself. Make it your ambition to gain understanding of the principles and thought processes that go into living a fulfilling, prosperous, and high-impact life. Once you understand the methods and principles, you can apply them to your personal life plan and make your goals unique to your own lifestyle, personality, and starting point.

God took billions of atoms to form you as a distinct person. You have unique characteristics, passions, goals, and vision that have a distinctive place in this world. You were specifically designed like a key to fit a single lock. How many times have we fumbled through a key ring to find the right fit, none of the keys are bad, they just fit unique and specific locks.

PERSONAL VISION COLLECTION

Over the years, I have gathered materials that I have found inspiring. In my personal collection, I have pages of inspirational quotes from great men and women that provide continuous encouragement for me. I have many personal development and executive self-assessment profiles. I also have pictures of orphanages and daycare centers I helped develop, so I can see the reality of the goals I have attained. There are also several personal notes from friends and loved ones and intimate goals I have yet to accomplish. This has helped me actualize my personal life convergence.

Life is a collision of unique gifts, passions, desires, and experiences that culminate in something that many have labeled convergence. Convergence is the point at which you are catapulted into your most important efforts. It is the amalgam of your unique self, gifting, training, and experiences. This combination creates a platform for our most rewarding and important accomplishments.

 3C EXERCISE

The *3C Companion Guide* (available for free at www.3cplan.org) has expanded material designed to give you space to develop a Life Action Plan.

- What defines your own personal fulfilment and prosperity?

- What important roles and relationships in your life create true fulfilment?

- Take the time to envision yourself in these situations as

though you were living in the future already. What character traits will you have to grow?

- What sort of nature and skill set will you have to have to live congruently with this new future self?

CHAPTER 10

PARTING THOUGHTS— GETTING READY FOR THE REST OF YOUR LIFE

"If you can't fly then run, if you can't run then walk, if you can't walk then crawl, but whatever you do you have to keep moving forward."
—MARTIN LUTHER KING JR

THE NEXT STEP

Your next step could possibly be one of the most important in your life. Henry Ford once said, "Whether you think you can or think you can't, you're right." It's the perseverance and the action to move forward, even with the existence of fear, anxiety, and doubt around us that makes the difference.

Make your priority those key elements that can bring about lasting, significant, and fulfilling change in your life. Avoid being at the mercy of other people's urgent requests. Think again about what priorities and principles are really substantial to you, and decide to engage in those things that are truly important. Just because something isn't urgent or screaming at you with a deadline, doesn't mean that it isn't one of the most important things in your life.

The three-circle strategy becomes the operating system for any plan in life. Whether you are wanting to focus on dieting, exercise, weight loss, entrepreneurial ventures, advancing in your company, strengthening your marriage, or growing your family, all of them require a plan, focus, skill, passion, and divine help or direction.

To drive this information deeper, buy this book for someone else as a gift and encourage them in the application of the material. This is not a veiled attempt at selling more books. I have honestly learned that trying to teach and convey material to others drives the information and meaning into a deeper level. I have tried my best to make the content, size, and price conducive to this being the kind of gift I personally would like to give or receive.

I also highly recommend attending one of our live events. These focus on: The

Three Circle Strategy for a Fulfilling Life, Time Management, Fulfilling your Destiny, and other important topics. These are held in various locations or on an individual basis to an organization. You can find out more about how to participate at www.DaveYarnes.com. The ability for you to be in a "live environment" to ask questions and get individual feedback as you plan your passion, chart your course, and own your life is incomparable. The interaction "band width" and interchange is invigorating at these live events.

When you face setbacks, remember that they are common parts of all of our lives. Make the choice to create a lifestyle that continually strives for the fulfilling, prosperous life you were designed to enjoy. Life can get busy and be filled with distractions. Without intentionality, the less important aspects (the cares, concerns, errands, and worries) can crowd out our focus on those things that truly matter.

It all comes down to choices, self-discipline, and self-control. As you move forward from here, make a commitment to yourself to never let those things that truly matter be at the mercy of those that don't. Plan your passion, chart your course, and own your life. More fulfilment and accomplishment than you have ever imagined begins now.

 **3C EXERCISE**

Getting ready for the Rest of Your Life

- What actions can you take to strongly begin new lifestyle changes?

- Which routines can you change to allow your 3C Strategy to grow strong roots right from the beginning?

Self-discipline can be the deciding factor between achieving deep, substantial change or superficial reorientation. How can you grow in this area?

The *3C Companion Guide* (available for free at www.3cplan.org) can be saved as a type of life journal once completed. It is designed to give you space to reflect and comment and has a printable format that can be stored and referenced. You can often refer back to track your progress and adjust your answers as your growth in the three circles continues for a lifetime. Be sure to write us at Info@DaveYarnes.com to share your breakthroughs. We enjoy reading your comments and feedback and helping with any questions as you plan your passion and chart your course to your fulfilling and prosperous life.

ABOUT THE AUTHOR

Dr. Dave Yarnes represents a unique voice in business today. He has been a serial entrepreneur for the last 30 years. He is in high demand as an executive coach, consultant, and keynote speaker. Dave's humor, candor, and spiritual insight paints a picture of business that is not often seen.

Reading this concise book is a great investment of time and energy.

—ROBERT WHITLOW
best-selling author of *A Time to Stand*

If you have any desire to grow in depth and power personally, professionally, and spiritually, *The Three Circle Strategy for a Fulfilling Life* is your guide. I know Dave Yarnes personally, and he is a remarkable entrepreneur and Christian leader who has established a profound blend of passionate spirituality and excellent business acumen. He brings a fresh perspective on how to live a full life and build the foundations for lasting prosperity.

—MIKE BICKLE
International House of Prayer
of Kansas City

Dave Yarnes' book is a wisdom-filled combination of spiritual and practical steps to make our careers fulfilling. We take Scripture at its word that God desires prosperity for His children. The question is how to then achieve that prosperity. Dave, with some 30 years of successful business to his credit, gives us a guide of how to do it. Characteristically, his *The Three Circle Strategy for a Fulfilling Life* begins with the Circle of Spirit. The Circle of Skill and the Circle of Self-Mastery follow. I highly recommend this book to those who wish to reach prosperity and do it God's way. From my 40 years of experience, I know that any time I followed the principles Dave outlines, I was successful. And any time I did not, my efforts led to failure. Now I know why.

—NICHOLAS F. S. PAPANICOLAOU
former majority shareholder and chairman
of Aston Martin Lagonda Group, UK

I highly recommend Dave Yarnes' new book, *The Three Circle Strategy for a Fulfilling Life*. I have known Dave for more than 20 years and have traveled and ministered with him on three continents. The field-tested insights on leadership unveiled in this book will change your life. Dave's chapter on the Circle of Self-Mastery is worth the price of the entire book. Thank you, Dave, for writing this much-needed book for the present and future generations of leadership.

—LARRY KREIDER, director of DOVE International

Rarely do I pick up a book these days that can hold me to the end without a break. But Dr. Dave Yarnes' *The Three Circle Strategy for a Fulfilling Life* is an exception to that rule.

With magnetic page-turning power, Dr. Yarnes packs tons of compelling wisdom within a powerful little book, written in an easy-to-follow writing style, that can change lives, if only the reader will heed its wisdom. The "Three Circle Strategy" of spirit, skill, and self-mastery is both revolutionary in thought and simplistically brilliant at the same time. It's as if the practical secrets to success in life have been there all along but made invisible by the thick fog of life's many distractions. The "Three Circle Strategy" is a bright sunbeam that removes the fog hiding those secrets.

Put another way, in a manner that is easy to digest and to grasp, Dr. Yarnes reveals the unique keys to personal success that have been there all along but yet are so hard to see because of the mundane clutter of life's distractions.

I predict that *The Three Circle Strategy for a Fulfilling Life* will become one of those power-packed "little books" that never leave your bedside, much like Napoleon Hill's classic *Think and Grow Rich* and Og Mandino's *The Greatest Salesman in the World*. The practical nuggets of truth for success and self-mastery within the three circles will become fountains of motivation and encouragement that will last a lifetime.

In the area of self-help, *The Three Circle Strategy for a Fulfilling Life* is destined to become a classic. I can't wait to give a copy to my son and am honored to wholeheartedly endorse it.

—Don Brown
author of the *Publishers Weekly* national best seller *The Last Fighter Pilot*, the Amazon national best sellers *Treason*, *The Malacca Conspiracy*, *Call Sign Extortion 17*, and Zondervan's Navy Justice Series

David Yarnes has a unique ability to approach any field and succeed by discovering the essential success formula hidden in it. What's great about Dave is that he does not teach others until he has mastered the craft himself. He has done this in more than one field—from mixed martial arts, to banking, to managing award-winning hotels, and now to mentoring organizations and leaders. He brings his unique gifts to us again in his most recent book, *The Three Circle*

Strategy for a Fulfilling Life, which is loaded with insights that can make the difference between mediocrity and mastery. I encourage you to buy this for yourself and for two or three friends. Tell them you would like to follow up with them and see what you all gleaned. You will be amazed at what you'll discover.

—DR. LANCE WALLNAU
founder of Lance Learning
Group in Dallas, Texas